I KNOW THE RULES

SCHOOL BUS

STOP

STOP

MARLA CONN

Rourke Educational Media

A Division of Carson Dellosa Education

Photo Glossary

 car

 classroom

 game

 **library**

 **lunchroom**

 **street**

High Frequency Words:
- I
- for
- know
- rules
- the

classroom

I know the rules for the **classroom**.

car

I know the rules for the **car.**

I know the rules for the **lunchroom.**

lunchroom

9

I know the rules for the **library**.

library

I know the rules for the **game.**

I know the rules for the **street**.

street

Activity

1. Go back to the story with a reading partner. Discuss how the children follow rules.

2. Share what rules you know for how to act in the car, in the classroom, while playing a game, in the library, in the lunchroom, and when crossing the street.

3. Create a cause-and-effect chart on the board and complete it with the class.

Cause	Effect
I want to learn and let others learn.	I follow the rules for the_____.
I want to be honest and win fairly.	I follow the rules for the_____.
I want to be safe from cars and dangers in the road.	I follow the rules for the_____.
I want to respect the driver.	I follow the rules for the_____.
I want to read my book and respect others.	I follow the rules for the_____.
I want my school community to have a peaceful lunch.	I follow the rules for the_____.